Shedding Our Grave Clothes

A Poetry Collection by David Greshel

Copyright © 2024 by David Greshel and Neon Sunrise Publishing

All rights reserved. No part of this book may be reproduced in any form or by any electronic or mechanical means, including information storage and retrieval systems, without the permission in writing from the publisher, except by a reviewer who may quote brief passages in a review.

This compilation contains some works of fiction. Locales and public names are sometimes used for atmospheric purposes. Any resemblance to actual people, living or dead, or to businesses, companies, events, institutions, or locales is completely coincidental. Any references to pop culture are owned by the specific companies and are not the property of the authors.

There are nonfiction poems included within that represent thoughts of the author. Any resemblance to actual events, locales, or persons, living or dead, is entirely coincidental.

ISBN: 978-1-961444-09-6

Art Credits – in order of appearance -

Image 1 – Chris Jones
Image 2 – Pixabay (no name)
Image 3 – Seth0s
Image 4 – Dimitris Vetsikas
Image 5 – Patty Jansen

Front Cover Original Photo – hurk
Back Cover Original Photo – Claudia Peters

Introduction

What is it like to be staring at the blank page and hoping the words will jump out of your brain and onto the screen with little to no effort from yourself? Maddening. Unproductive. Depressing. So, essentially, writing.

Ok, maybe that's a bit reductive and one-sided, but I have to imagine you've felt that way yourself if you have spent any amount of time producing words on paper (digital characters on an input device?) No? Just me?

Shedding Our Grave Clothes serves as a testament to four years' worth of wrestling with the beasts of procrastination and writer's block; four years of chasing the muse through the same thematic streams and pictures to produce some memorable moments and wonderful lines. There is no one single theme or binding thread beyond my own voice and yet I hope that people will take away the ideas and images evoked in this collection's title. It's meant to recall a feeling of rebirth and resurrection, of the shedding of old skins and ideals in favor of something new.

If this is the first work of mine that you've picked up – welcome! You've got a veritable jukebox of emotional output ready to carry you from the fresh start of 2020 through to the end of 2023.
If you're a repeat visitor, welcome to the latest and greatest on our expanding poetry tour.

I appreciate you all and hope you enjoy the ride!

See you where the sidewalk ends,

David Greshel – June 2024

Acknowledgements/Thank Yous

There are a lot of things that go into bringing a book to life. While Neon Sunrise is pretty much a one-man show behind the scenes, this book (and all the others) would not be possible without the love and support of my family and friends who have encouraged me and been the sounding board for the work now before you.

My deepest gratitude to each and every one of you.

An extra special 'thank you' to the following people who supported the Kickstarter project and helped bring this volume to life:

Travis Gibb
Jonathan Hedrick
Vulpecula
Kasey Sargent
Heidi Hess
Joel Gonzalez
Bret Eayrs
Jan-Michael Turla
Joanne Williams
Johnny Jensen
Genna Perugini
Dr. Kristin Wallace
Matt Knowles & Steph Cannon (Insymmetry Creations)

2020

Listening to the Dreams of January

Sparks flicker in the shadow of memory
Awakening dormant imaginings
Latent feelings thought swept away
Now shimmer on the surface
And lead me to a moment of solitude
Contemplating every implication
Floating between synapses
Watching the wafting wisps of stem
Rising from the warming vitality
Found in the first morning cup
On the first day of a dawning new year
Brimming with unrivaled potential
And the growing luminescence of hope
To light this path of possibility

Apocalypse Express, Overnight to Everywhere

Stolen atoms split and bleed
Melting in the ensuing reaction
That erupts outward in annihilation
Of everything we came to know before
Bleaching bone and ash
In the onslaught of nuclear winter
Beyond the scape of dreams

This wasn't the intended outcome
Of our misbegotten revolutions
But rebellion is a currency
Spent on short-fused reactionaries
Intoxicated by evaporating youth
And the piper's seasick lullaby

We only wanted someone to hear us
To acknowledge the actuality
That was so blindingly obvious
Even the skies were screaming
One note panic ever out of key

Silence fell beneath the lightning
Scorched in the twilight reply
With no apologies left to whisper
No obituaries to immortalize

__Immortality in Ways Hitherto Undreamed Of__

We never danced the same way twice
Choosing different rituals by starlight
And singing lost hymns to passing nebulae
Encircling a celestial sea beyond this galaxy
Balanced on the tip of a sharpened quill
Raven black with obsidian ink to match
That flows from a hidden wellspring
Of infinite dreams held in temple vessels
Embellished in runes of onyx and amber
Enchanted in the rhyme of spells
And the dulcet tones of silver bells
Let forth to serenade the unfolding horizon
With mystic poetry
And a rosy crucifixion tune
That recalls a captivating passion shared
Angelic and demonic entwined in bliss
And it's all just a clever bit of deception
A very fantastic distraction
From our solitary match of suicide bingo
And the unending infamy of electric delusion
At the impending end of everything

Simple Silly Rhyme

Sunsets shimmering silently
Winding into the end of daylight
With a languid bit of flair
To set the stage for twilight
And the awakening of night

Never Let a Good Crisis Go to Waste

I've been listening all the while
Bewildered by the fever pitch
Unadulterated on the party line
And stoking the flames of panic
That erupt at the slightest spark
Tucked within imagined whisperings

All that unending noise reverberates
Careening through my thoughts
As I try desperately to align them
In the light of realistic outcomes
But the screeching alarm
Is irreconcilable to the solidity
Of what I know to be true

I will not be goaded into fear
Won't be driven by doomsayers
Salivating for your next click
And baiting another hook

I am more
Than some target demographic

Living Left on the Dial

The speed of life oscillates wildly
Twenty years past in a blink
Yet it seemed like March might never end
Ebb and flow are constant
Built on broken stones of change
Eroded in the misty-eyed nostalgia
I've come to crave on moonless nights
Where the only answer offered
Is to run like hell in high water
Through the quicksand left behind
Caught in the whisper of a moment
I can't stop thinking about
The one that led you to disappear
Without fanfare or salutations
And it's only a song for the lonely now

I Believed it to be Sweet, No Matter the Name

I can't remember exactly when
It may have come to pass
But somewhere in the echo it was decided
That this breakneck speed of life
Was the standard we had to meet
That we had to measure up to lightning
To be worthy of the thunder

I'm so tired of trying to fly
With these imaginary wings
Yearning for a spirit of rest
And the scent of roses on your neck
Inhaled in the warmth of our embrace

Tempted to Dream about Hot August Nights

Stuck in a perception of immobility
Left to wander through these waves
Of memory and illusion
Dwelling on idle thoughts of travel
And the highway siren serenade

Remembering that summer road trip
West on unthought backroads
Winding from Chicago to Los Angeles
Stopping at lost legends
And gawking at decaying attractions

I fell in love with a waitress
Daydreaming in a forgotten diner
Sharing cigarettes and spare change
I wrote her a letter every day
Silly romantic nothings never sent
And I wonder where she is these days
Did she ever find her true way home

The song fades out
Last number on the A-side
Flip the record and start again
Drifting further out
Into tides of lovesick nostalgia

One day I might even open the letters
Remember what it was like to dream of love
On the wings of an envelope and the price of a stamp
Recall all the nights in desecrated phonebooths
Romancing your answering machine with soulful songs
When I knew you were working
Hoping for the day you might finally escape
That dead-end destitution
And somehow end up on my doorstep

One day I might even recognize
I imagined all of this
Watching you stare out that truckstop window
Lost in thought
Coffee and cigarettes carrying you
Through one last break before the dinner shift

And I never even got your name
But you're forever imprinted on my memoriam

I've Heard it Both Ways

It's always been a bit like charades
Blindfolded in the dark
Balanced on the edge of a cliff
Trying to guess the pantomimed idiom
And the extent of this enigma
Offered up like a golden alibi

We know it's a kind of game
The sort with enamored implications
And the promise of enlightenment
On the shores of new frontiers
Out beyond the reach of humanity
Hanging on the fringes of divinity

Effigies and Voodoo Dolls

The exhilaration takes hold in waves
Catapulting our heroes to undreamt levels
And onto unsought (?) heights of divinity
Prescribing roles not meant to be grasped
In the slippery grip of humanity
We carve them into imperfect idols
Saddled with our lofty ideologies
Misaligned and undesired
A receptacle for our adulation…

At least until the façade begins to crack
Revealing creatures of flesh and blood
Subject to the same sins as everyone
And we scream and wail our discontent
How dare they betray our worship
With their shortcomings?!

Another casualty of popular opinion
Led to the firing line for abject failure
As an ill-conceived deity
Leaving us with self-inflicted scars
Searching for the next martyr to burn

What was it You Wished For?

I remember that it felt like floating
At least in the opening moments
Tumbling down a verdant hillside
With the melody of your laughter
Caressing my ears
Followed by my own
As I watched you follow suit
Until we were both entangled
In love with the warmth
Of both sunlight and flesh enmeshed
Wishing we could lie here
Just lie here
Watching cloudless blue skies
Deepen to darkest indigo
Counting stars and passing planes
Dreaming it would never fade

And I remember…

Asphyxiation and Retribution

This weariness is vampiric
Exsanguinating every drop of life
From this flesh and bone
Sick to death of wondering
How unbidden shades of melanin
Are a valid notion
For determining a person's worth
Or right to exist
How we seem to so easily accept
A willing blindness to suffering
To maintain such shallow comfort

We did not ask to paint ourselves
In the palette of our birth
Nor do we inherit hatred
Upon our exit from the womb
And it's beyond time
For such antiquarian atrocities
To be resigned to the pages of history
As I am so very tired of reliving
These broken tragedies
In the faces of my brethren
And hearing the anguish
Tearing through their voices

What Comes After Lovesick Lullabies

I am the sanguine night
Swirling in between somber shadows
Dripping into the rising horn lines
And staccato guitar riffs
That howl the oppression of the blues
At the unblinking faceless orb
Rising to dominate the darkened sky

I am the whispered desire
Tumbling from trembling lips
In stolen illicit moments
Beyond the ravenous gaze
Of a tabloid lothario
And the covetous rage
Of former lovers

I am the song you can't forget
Pulsing with a living melody
Exploding from every verse
I am the dust on the highway
Carried south on autumn winds
I am the words you never said
Left in the annals of 'might've been'

That First Track is a Killer

The heat slides out into the evening
Clinging to humid accolades
Without even a hint of cooling shade
In the arms of our summer sauna
Where another Tuesday unfolds
Entwined in addictive melodies
Spiraling out of another game of mixtape roulette
Where a twist of the unknown
Hits every note just right
And we singalong
Bleeding out at the top of our lungs
And knowing every single word
That tells the story we want to be
Echoed in guitars and power chords

Flip the tape and let's go again
One more song
One more dance
It's just what we need tonight

She Said it's the Only Way to Fly

What was the last thing to catch your mind
And captivate your inner dialogue?

What were the whisperings you heard
In the corners we dared not gaze upon?

Is it just a brush with the hand of madness
Or has it sunk its talons in deep?
Are the voices framed in unison
Or is the dissonance keeping you from sleep?

Is the white knight still talking backwards
With a tea party in full swing
Or did the delusions finally subside
Into your familiar fever dream?

This game of questions has no apparent end
Nor is there much hope of enlightenment
At the bottom of the empty inkwell

Pyromania Expressed in the Language of Desire

I embraced the enveloping inferno
Bathing in an unwavering wildfire
That rages across shifting paradigms
In which I chased after the warmth
But fell in love with the pain
And I can trace the tracks of scars
Burned into wooden memories
That recall my former loves
And highlight fallen shadows
Stretching into storied nights
Alive in the sound of revolution
Screaming sordid soliloquies
And dreaming in the wake of delirium
Where only the dance remains
That sweeps us into stolen spotlights
And I embrace the raging inferno…

Declarations and Guthrie Tunes

There's a celebration in the air
Exploding in colored showers
That deafen and glitter back to earth
And the metaphor is not lost on me
As I reflect on another fourth of July

My Grandfather's birthday
For the record

And I know I'm not any sort of patriot
But I still love this land
My America and all it's supposed to be
I still believe in her ideals
Even though they're a bit hidden
In the midst of such heavy sadness

But I believe in the home of the brave and free
Where all humanity is created equal
And I refuse to rest until that belief becomes reality
When all our bloody history
Will finally be resigned to the past
And we can all sing along with Woody

"This land is your land…this land is my land…"

The Substance of Soul Surfing

Staring out into the endless expanse
Dreaming of dying stars in supernova
And the silent horror in the vacuum
As the implosion signals an ending
That I watched unfold in slow motion
Erupting in an event horizon
Until nothing remained
But the cold dark infinite
Engulfing everything in its wake
And there is no escape
No course of action but surrender

…am I still dreaming…or have I crossed into the yawning void?

If We Wanted to Trade Lines, We'd have Gone to Hollywood

All those years of tobacco smoke
Left their subtle stench to linger
In the cracked and yellowed paint
Very much the same way the whisky
Has left its poison fingerprints
On the surface of my liver
But I don't regret a single night we spent
Trading shots and stories at the bar
Watching all the shameless suitors fall in
Hoping they might just have a clever line
Or at the very least a winning smile
I think I may even remember the replies
Because it never hurt you to fall from heaven
And you had no phone number to share
Except Jenny's from the bathroom
I never did quite understand the tactics
Of this meat market dancefloor jungle
Replete with failed Alpha metaphors
And dimestore jukebox heartthrobs
Bent on winning the night
Despite what your feelings might've been
And all you truly wanted
Was a genuine interest in the guts you spilled
And the dreams you shared
Not a conquest
A friendship on which to build

Titanic Meet Iceberg

I suppose it's worth mentioning
That this was the exact moment
When it all slipped through
The grasp of tired fingers
Exploding in shattered pieces
And other clever metaphors
That paint the broken nature
Of what we once shared

It's also worth mentioning
Upon such pointed reflection
How much blood we spilled
How many tears we shed
In service of reconciliation
Despite the mounting evidence
Of an impending collapse

It's worth mentioning
If you feel like keeping score

Spirit Walks with Obsidian Panthers

The disbelief is overwhelming
How can such devastating events
Exist in the space of our minds
Simultaneously invading
Our conscious attention

We struggle to uphold
The soul of a nation
Drowning in partisan narratives
And a unified directive
Is a voice lost in the churning sea

We mourn the life of a man
Who embodied the heart of a king
One we'd have followed
Into the very jaws of death
And a passage beyond the end

This liquid darkness is maddening
Painting everything in shadow
Light will crest the horizon
Though it's so very hard to see
Standing within sight of hell

Selling the Story to Anyone Listening

There are so many words I can say
Descriptions I could rattle off freely
Truth or fiction being of little bearing
For the practiced speech I'm breathing
Subtle nuances in the art of deception
Make for the coldest callous phrases

So, of course I can hurl the cruelest barbs like
"I don't love you"
"I'm glad we're finished"
"I never want to see you again"

Say them?
Sure

That doesn't at all account for the daggers
I swallow with every uttered syllable
And the open grave my throat has become
At this attempt to divorce my thoughts from my feelings
To salve some of the pain
In the fact that I don't mean a single word
And I've been stuck inside my own head
Since the moment you pulled the 'chute

Don't Start Having Your Own Opinions Now, We Were Getting On So Well...

I guess I thought we'd be past all this by now
That somehow we'd have figured out
Just how small hatred really is
A tiny speck of nothing
Screaming into a megaphone
And begging for a prolonged gaze
In its direction

And yet we keep feeding the little bastard
Watching it magnify and multiply
Invading public discourse as a talking point
On every media teleprompter
Perpetuating a cycle of paranoid pyromania
Where we'd rather incinerate our own
Before considering how we might benefit
From another point of view

I really thought it must be time
To give love a try
To open minds and hearts and ears
To the unvoiced experiences we've not known
To the pain and plight of our shared flesh

Apparently I'm a bit ahead in the story
The rest of this lot is still lost
In bloody politics and tribal animosity
And I'm so very tired of waiting for them
To finally come to terms with the plot

A Waltz Unremembered

It's a weird thing
The ghosts we chase
The phantoms we attempt to resurrect
On the assumptions this life is better
Than where their journey has taken them
A kind of empathetic selfishness
Born in the throes of grief

It's not that we want to keep them here
In the midst of their suffering
Or that we ascribe ourselves in deity
We just want an alternative experience
One that doesn't involve such pain
Or such an early exit

That's the mystery though, isn't it?
The unseen gamble of the living
Banking on aces and eights
We always want more time at the end
When there was so much story
To live along the way

I just want one more dance with you
One more day in the light
One last chance to tell you
All of the 'I love yous'
I never got to say

Castaway Calling Cards

Crystal coastline shimmering softly
A jewel in the morning sunlight
And a view undreamt of
After days adrift on unforgiving seas

Washed ashore at high tide
Clutching fistfuls of wet sand
And breathing ragged hallelujahs
Before passing out in the blaze of noon

Awakened to alien soundscapes
And the anxiety of the unseen
Still dreaming of familiar fauna
And a memory of mundane myopia

Afloat on the River Lethe

I left my body behind on that sullen shore
Climbed aboard this tiny ferry
For reasons I can't quite recall
And the boatman hasn't said a word
Steering us downriver toward the misty shoals
A destination unchosen
And I'm haunted by her face
With a beauty that aches
Floating below the troubled surface
Alluring and unconcerned
Beckoning me to drink deep
While her name dances on my tongue
Flickers in the synapse of memories
That vanish with each passing sip
And yet I can't forget those eyes
The dangerous kind that pierce my very essence
Burning away the last vestiges of all I ever was
Enveloping me into her entropic embrace
To rest eternal in the sweetness of oblivion

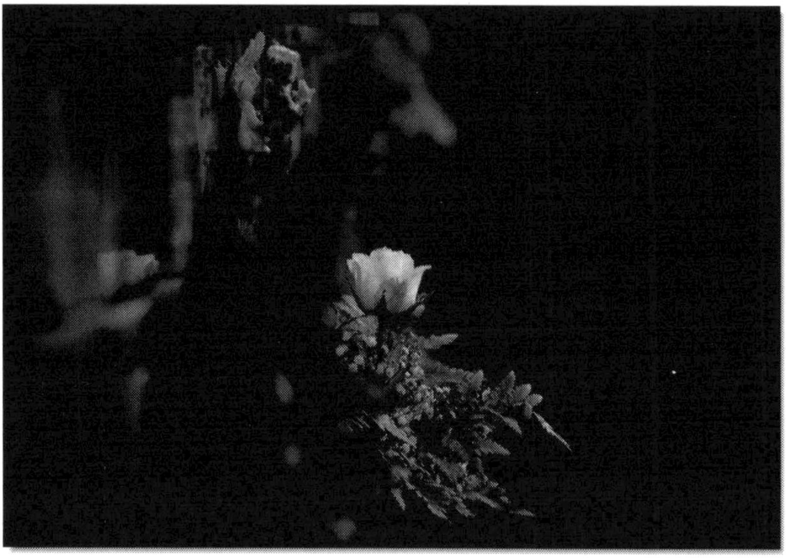

2021

Lucky Strikes and Last Rites

I find it funny since I don't smoke
But these nights seem tailor-made
For the scratchy drag of cigarettes
And a rolling summer thunderstorm
That I watch from a 3rd floor balcony
Lulled by the rhythm of raindrops
And punctuated rumbling
Exhaling alternate breaths
Of unwanted ghosts and regrets
That smell of cheap love
And cheaper booze
Wrapped in a haze of menthol
Illuminated in streaks of lightning
That shatter the obsidian sky
Leaving me with the unfiltered ashes of these thoughts
And a bed full of unbidden memories

Epiphany in Sight of a Noose

One week past
And I still find myself dismayed
Returning to a picture of the gallows
Ominously erected on the Capitol lawn
A hungry symbol of murderous intent
Underscoring the dangerous fantasies
Of zealots and madmen

Did you really think you'd be hailed as heroes by the masses?
That we'd all somehow wake up
From your perceived delusion
Once those "traitors" were swingin' in the wind?

The smoke rolls through the streets
Washing over the stench
Of your violent futility
Claiming self-styled revolutionaries
Choking on the bitter pill of consequence
At the hand of narcissistic vanity

Drawing a Blank on the Million Dollar Question

The chill of darkened shadow
Creeps along the barren walls
Of this hollowed well
That once hid a flowing spring
That bubbled and rose in season
But has long since fallen to disuse and evaporation
A relic of another age

Imagination pinwheels wildly
Spinning through blackened corners
In search of deconstructed thoughts
And listening for the lilting muse
Whose song once thundered
Now reduced to a whisper of memory
That lingers in the waves of an echo
A glimmer of a former life

Dreaming a New Take on Living

The morning exhales
Releasing the whispered hope of dawn
On the crest of the eastern horizon
Dripping rivulets of golden light
Through half-closed bedroom curtains
And signaling another new day
To one not quite ready to begin
Still caught in the tendrils of dreaming
Reliving a treasured Spring evening
From an adolescent year long past
When the world seemed much smaller
And all that mattered was this moment
Lying beneath the starlight
Wishing on the ones that fell to earth
Until it fades into darkness
Interrupted by sunlight and cacophony
And the ritual of waking

Grade A Plans and Punch Out Routines

First breath in the awakening fallout
Sputtering and wheezing
Testing the poisoned metallic residue
Left hanging on murder winds
That scream through disintegration ballads
And I recognize the language of dreams
Telegraphed in nightmare cryptography
Leaving me speechless
Dumbfounded

I thought I knew all the words to this one
All the strongest phrases
And clever rhymes
Yet now I'm barely staggering
Clutching for familiar time
In some semblance of a proper key
That betrays my sinking confidence
Revealing a startling lack
Of anything that might be believable

Blues in the Key of Picasso

I live in the lines I wrote for you
Breathing between syllables
Stretching to fill familiar harmonies
With a hope of feeling your melody
Softly gliding through the mental static

The siren of memory holds court in your absence
Reveling in rose tinted nostalgia
Whispering incantations in forgotten tongues
And making a game of my wondering
The kind I never had much of a chance to win

Left to the folly of my own devices
I throw an unforgettable party
For all the heartbreak
That's left me living in the lines I wrote for you
Ordering room service
Dreaming of another hotel year
And the howl of a dying guitar

A Worldly Riff for Jimmy

We danced through foreboding showers
Aloof to any sense of oncoming anxiety
So long as the melody never wavers
And the waltz remains in fashion

Weren't we happy then?

Turning circles in tired rhythms
And waiting for the prowling wine leopard
Bearing gifts of Rose and Pinot Noir
To wash the night away

If not then, when?

Spring showers linger into the dawn light
Cascading prisms on golden horizons
Tracing between sleeping and waking
Fighting for the promise of either

Can you still feel them fluttering?

Cycles and Circles or Some Such Thing

It's almost imperceptible at first
The subtle shift in the narrative
Where grief subsides for a moment
And something new awakens
The firs sprouts of Spring
Amongst the surrounding decay
A metaphor for balance
A picture of how we bloom to rot
With the growth in our own lives
Happening much the same
New revelations appearing
In the wake of challenged paradigms

Who I was
Who I am
Who I will become

All entwined in this journey of being
Bound up in the glory of living

A Left Turn at Albuquerque

What mysteries can still be seen
Here in the kingdom of light
Illuminated by pulsing radiance
Beneath the gaze of an eternal sun
Pushing silvered shadows into memory
Deep in the recesses of recollection
Past the place where missing things go
And the isle of stolen dreams
To rest on the fringes of oblivion
Where we're left to wonder
What mysteries can still be seen…

No One Sits by the Phone Anymore

The sparks flicker and dance
Sporadically sputtering in earnest
Hoping to catch the right tinder
And set the night ablaze

Recalling what was said between us
That read like post mortem philosophy
Trailing a fading echo of a stolen moment
From a life worth living
Long absent in this present predicament
That bears all the recent scars
Of two people torn asunder

Begging off the price of forgetting
In all these repetitions bleeding through
The saddest songs on the stereo
And the bottom of another whiskey sour

"It's Alright We Told You What to Dream"

The hours between last call and dawn
Often strike a dreadful tone
Overrun with unfulfilled wants
Unsatisfied desires
Questions of self-illumination
Or lack thereof
Invade these lonely minutes
And leave me desperate
Clinging to a modicum of rest
Reaching towards the solace of dream
That slips so callously past
Dissolving into the clarion of morning
And the empire of the sun

X-Ray Parables

I can see the wheels turning
The steam rising
All the cheeky responses at the ready
As the inquiry buds and blooms
Against a tide of immaturity
Yet it cannot be denied
So we're gonna let it roll

When's the last time you were naked?
And I don't mean uncovered
For cleansing or for pleasure
Or any other reason you might imagine
I mean naked
Raw and vulnerable
Exposed and laid bare
Stripped of every erected façade
In the hope of deepest intimacy

Have you ever ben truly naked?

Armchair Philosophy Acrobatics

Mesmerized
Gliding through hollow memories
Tucked between the ticking seconds
Watching the gilded watch swing
Entranced in metronomic aspirations

Hypnotized
Tracing tiled tessellations
In exponential sets
Exploratory dance steps
We follow by feel

Galvanized
Mortality in motion
Exploding through pinholes
Light-years from everywhere
In the span of a single breath

A Trade of Donuts for Dollars

We are a study in contrast
Painted scarlet in an ivory tomb
Exposing truth in the heart of a lie
Believing punctuated silences
Fastened to the tale of a rhyme
Learning all the best showtunes
On the lips of a talkative mime
Spinning manufactured outrage
On the heels of a vacancy sign
Burning books just to read them
Stealing time from a broken hourglass
Shining darkness in the rising sun

We are a paradox unimagined
Existential and overrun

It's Brilliant in my Head

It's a prickly sort of thing
Balanced on the wings of providence
And soaked in the vitality of possibility
Catching us in the space between
The friendship and the fear
With me wanting to play things so cool
But overthinking every angle
Until I end up saying nothing at all
When I just want to shout about
How you're like the one song
I never tire of listening to
The pages and lines I recite
The emotions I profess in rhyme
You are the air in my lungs
The first thought in my mind
And it all passes in a blink
Leaving us on the in-between
Stroking silent serenades
On the fringe of might've been

Another Page in Your Book

Waiting
Endlessly waiting

For the new earth to rise
For another soul design
For the old vices to subside
For the renewal of minds

Epiphany of the morning
Eureka on the tongue
From a golden revelation
And an everyday apocalypse

Waiting
Endlessly waiting

Never Speaks of Nothing in Nightmare

That first moment when your eyelids crack
And morning filters in
The one before any indication
Of impending bliss or tribulation

What's that lie for you?

Are you wrapped up and cocooned
Safe in the warmth of your slumber?

Commanding the queen-sized solo
Or entangled in the limbs of another?

Do your dreams speak of fairy blessings
Or leave you haunted and begging for respite?

Are you comfortable in the arms of the night?

I haven't been since the last time I saw you take flight…

An Allusion Afterglow

Sand
Tiny granule amassed
Stretching outward
Omnidirectionally
A desert eternal
Though I hoped for a beach

It seems like eons have passed
Bleached and blistered
An erosion artist redesign
Of this grand façade
With no escape in sight

This wasn't our desired destination
Nor the height of any list
We sought after the afterlife
With no intention of dying
Just a whisper and a glimpse

It's all Swings and Roundabouts

I made a serious attempt in the unwinding evening to listen for my own heartbeat…to push past the white noise of existence and drown out the auditory pollution that hangs all around me…not just to feel my pulse but to hear that swelling rhythm rushing through my ears…to slow down enough that blood and breath are the loudest constants…if but for a few moments before the enticing distractions reclaim my attention span and crack me like a Thanksgiving wishbone…a fractured tug o' war parlor trick I'm too dazzled to evaluate in any real sense and so I lay here in the unfolding arms of the night and try to pick out the thunder of my own heartbeat…

Grounded and Restless

Strange
The things you find yourself longing for
In the grip of isolation

I never though to miss the sight
Of arrivals and departures
Baggage claim and safety checkpoints
The thrill of takeoff and a plane in flight

Never thought to miss the sound
Of air brakes and mechanical doors
The rhythmic clacking of tracks on trestles
And the countryside gliding past
In the streak of a bullet train

Never thought to miss the feeling
Of open highways and mountain roads
The rush of air and the Clash on the stereo
Miles devoured in the dead of night
Cross-country road trip
In a borrowed automobile

Will it ever feel the same?

The Pulse Unbroken

I found solace in the thunderstorm
The way the rain danced on the windows
And the lightning crawled across the sky
Minimized the internal tension
The anxiety begging for attention
Melting back into the rumbling distance
Left to breathe
To listen

Daybreak saunters in
Bisecting shadows
Reflecting golden radiation
Across acres of calm
Outside my windowsill
And a Bird of Paradise unfolds
Resplendent in orange and violet

Life hums
Life abides

...and Now a Word from Our Sponsors

We tend not to speak of failures
At least not in any way constructive
Preferring to excise and redact
Those inconvenient details
The kind of historical revisionism
Wielded by acolytes who lust for power
They could never hope to see
Let alone control
But we're all victors here
Perched atop this teetering mound
Of freezing ash and bleached bone
Deflecting decades of decay
With the shining promises
Of our own self-important greatness

Speaking of Sleeping Standing Up

It would almost be funny
To see you in the here and now
With all the practiced malice
And the careful pattern of deceit you still cling to
Clenched in a fist of misplaced rage
And a tight-lipped plastic smile
That hides a mouth bent on war and decimation

A caricature of all the nightmare cliches
A pathetic pantomime
And yet you still think
You're the pinnacle of fright
But you're nothing more than the wisp of a reflection
Unworthy of a mention
Left to the scraps of solar flares
Forgotten and haunted

Somewhere this is Directed at Me

The thoughts that tumble free in the midst of this rumination aren't the most profound…they're littered with cheeseball smiles and tired metaphors underpinning poignant feelings that are often only expressed to a silent mirror…and despite all of that there is simply not enough life left to live where it makes sense to keep holding it in…So I'll scream these words 'til my lungs burst…I will love you like the waves love the shore until the last tide is swallowed by the sea…until the last stars burn out in the ebony night and leave us wishing on a memory…I will love you through the last waltz around the supernova of the sun…until our final breath escapes into the failing atmosphere…I will love you like the laughter of children and the first taste of hot chocolate on Christmas morning…like the smell of God fresh after the rain…through all the endings and new beginnings…the fabled fairytale reciprocities…I still love you with every tortured lyric and tattooed scar decorating my pounding heart…I will love you despite the silence and the absence…the sort only we two can comprehend…I will love you…I do love you…always and forever…je t'aime…

Hopelessly Devoted Rushing In

I played the jester once
Though I much preferred the bard
Dealing in flashes of brilliance
And an adventure in song
To the fire eating juggler
With a joke and a rhyme

Yes, I played the fool
How could I not?

We were always on this path
Star-crossed and predestined
Bound for the yellowed pages
Of a 'stranger than fiction' tell-all
And the movie of the week

Despite the looming futility
I went to war and bled for you
Sacrificed my prime
And in my pain I promised you tomorrow
Like I spoke for days and seasons

Yes, I am a fool
The question is, whose?

Chasing White Whales in Toy Sailboats

Somewhere in the distance it shimmered
An unknown anomaly refracting daylight
In ways that can't be ignored
Never getting any closer
Never changing in scope
It just glittered out on the edge
Beckoning to overactive imaginations
Baited hook, line, and sinker

We sailed out in search of answers
Sought solace in the disappearing sun
Chasing the glitch on the horizon
Losing our dreams one by one
Still we persisted in defiance
Immortal 'til the quest is done
Sharing space with famous monsters
Breaking monkeys with money and guns

A question hangs in our minds
What about tomorrow?
We're off the map
With no land in sight
And Leviathan unbound
Waiting to devour

'Looking Back on Today' was Never Our Song

Skyward sonatas serenade in solitude
The drifting voices finding harmony
In equal parts aligned in rhyme
That lend themselves to meditation
And other subtle attempts
To soothe more savage reactions

Really, what more could I have done?
I've replayed the scenarios a thousand times
Looking for answers that don't exist
Or pages I might've missed
To explain the current outcome
And this gnawing hole in my chest

'I painted your name on my bones'
Knit you into my inner being
To keep your ghost contained
Bound our souls to a fading memory
That last number on our jukebox
And the comfort of a fallen night

We Blistered in Our Own Sun

Ya know, they called it an Indian summer but I never for the life of me quite understood why…but I remember the heat…borderline oppressive…hanging in the air like a shimmer that you only half believe is there…humid as a sauna you can't seem to leave no matter how much you might try…it left us restless and hungry…begging for the slightest hint of an ocean breeze from the coast we once knew…days fade to nights without any real difference beyond the color and the lighting…clocks tick on at a loss of purpose…I remember the heat…the fire that burned between us…left us scorched and smoldering…unwilling to concede to the ashes…and it was only a summer lived a lifetime ago…but I remember the heat…

We Didn't Dance and There was No Moonlight

The lightning in the distance
A nice touch of the ominous
If a bit overdone in the starless ebony
Recalled in horror themed introductions
And that lone flickering streetlight
Losing its shine to hungry shadows
While everything within just screams
To run in any other direction

We all find our way to the crossroads
Contemplate the face of the devil alone
Wondering at the nature of the bargain
And this heart made of glass and stone

Preferably Who or Feelgood

There was another one this morning
Swirling in the mists before sunrise
The unmistakable twinkle of your eyes
And the curve of your smile
Dissipating in the rising summer heat

I suppose it could be cute
The inescapable nature of it all
You're everywhere
In every cloud and tree
Floating in the cereal bowl
And on the cover of tempting magazines

Is it harmless?
This notion of pareidolia
Or is it obsession?
Dragging me deeper into psychosis
With every new perception

Is there a Doctor in the house?

Explaining Consequences to Gremlins

Ashes are all that remain
A dirty snowfall covering this field
That was once a forest
Dotted with dying embers
And a memory of towering trees

We can't help but stare
Trying to wrap our minds
Around this combustible decimation
Whispering a prayer like the moon
Rising to the lonesome howls

Wasted Youth Re-examined

Call it a story if it helps
An imaginative fiction
A clever cover-up
Meant to misdirect
This futuristic fabrication
(Oh, just call it a lie)

I may spin a tale or two
And I've sung more than a few
Without malice or ill intent
But you're never satisfied
With these lengthy litanies

We're drowning in the ink
Of all these unread pages
Both too proud to consider
The other's true potential
Despite aggressive diatribes
Screaming to the contrary

I Never Listen to the Radio Anymore

Signals on the switchboard
Vying for attention
Each one a vocal opinion
From an eager admirer
Long time listener, first time caller
Excited to overshare
And underwhelm
Reciting diatribes from suspect sources
Expanding the extreme dissonance
Of our national experience

I just wanted to know
If you were taking requests
And now I'm aware of
The state of your union
(and the health of your colon)

Is it too late to ask
For Panama by Van Halen?

When All Signs Point to 'No"

We like to play these games
Sometimes without even knowing it
Buried within our psyches
Balanced on the edge of a dream

You know the ones I mean
The measured avoidance
The alternate phrases
The door left open just a crack
For future opportunities
Or fallback possibilities

We don't like the finality of it
A period bringing a halt
To our extended sentence
The implications of commitment
Behind a line in the sand

Even with that in the air
There's no leaving here
Without the closure
Of this spoken word

(breathes)

Goodbye.

Couch Surfing in Soul Sessions

It's worth mentioning that I'm not always a willing participant in these exercises of self-reflection and I would often rather spend time doing anything else instead of another long look at motives and internal directives…growth doesn't just happen in a vacuum but if we could avoid the extra layers of bad decisions to shed I wouldn't mind the change…yes, this hurts…I'd be suspicious if it didn't…and while I might prefer something easy and mindless it's necessary to engage in this process or else I find that where I leave myself is in the constricting arms of apathy…held close but far from safe and blind to all the steps I've made…

The Music's Never Over and Our Light is Eternal

I've often wondered at length
If you think I don't remember
All the moments we've captured
The inseparable nature
Of entire summers spent entwined
Or the burning brilliant inferno
Encased in our winter embrace

In what world would I ever forget you?
The touch of your slender tips
Gliding across my skin
Like fingered strings on a violin
Lingering in perfect time

No, I remember every one
Flickering on the home movie memory reel
Reciting them back
In the lines of our favorite films
Writing this poem of us
On the flesh of our pounding hearts
And in the breath of this unending kiss

Last Stop 'til Thunderdome

I just can't anymore
Words that leave a hollow sound
And a hint of death on the tongue
Percolating in the steaming morass
Of what we never quite achieved
Only sort of believed
Bu still held out for the hope
Floating with messages in bottles
To illuminate our shared experience

Of course, that was before
We tripped over the weight of ego
And ran out of the slightest evens
Settled in the dust of remember whens
Built on the backs of never again
And the whispers of might've been

Exhausting
That's the simplest descriptor
And the truest
(if honesty is what we're aiming for)

This dance we've found ourselves in
Tiresome and repetitive
A pugilistic pantomime
Undersold and overhyped
And I'm tired…so tired…

At least let me dream it the way it's meant to be

A Poseur by any Other Name

The warming air of morning
Interrupts the ambient comfort
And signals the rise of another day
Replete with fashionable talking points
And clever hashtag heroics
A starving cry for relevancy
On a landscape of haute couture hysterics
And imaginary bloodbaths
That scream for the undivided attention
Of keyboard clerics and wind-up soldiers
Marching to the media fife
But only to the edge of the shadows
Flirting with the taste of the ideals
Without all that baggage of commitment
And another cause is just a click away

Maybe this one will generate more traffic

Petitioning the Court of Morpheus

For just a moment there was something cognizant in the wake of shifting memories…a kind of mutual recognition in the shared dreamscape we choose to inhabit in that span between dusk and dawn…travelling light years in rapid-eye movement real estate in search of I can't quite remember what that hangs out on the tip of my tongue and just out of reach in all but the last lucid instant before consciousness returns us to the daylight with only the faintest recollection of another life in the endless kingdom…and we lie there wondering which was more real…until the tedium claims us and we anxiously wait for the next chance to journey beyond the wall of sleep…

Eraser Nubs and Worn Out Delete Keys

It becomes a kind of taunt
The flashing cursor
The blank page
Expectantly waiting to be filled
And spark the next enlightenment
But there's nothing in the bucket

An empty well
A broken pen

It's not for lack of trying
Nor a loss for words
More like a stifling sense of mediocrity
And a jaded "case of the Mondays"
Wrapped in the dull sheen of 'meh'

Sometimes the muse is silent
Waiting in the dawning dream
Sometimes they're hoarse from screaming
To a crowd of deafened ears

Welcome Package Retrospective

There's blood in this sunrise
Painting the skies in crimson
Preceding another Summer squall
That leaves me sullenly sodden
On the receding shore
Building monuments to memories
For no one but me
Awkward reminders of the recent past
Weighing like invisible anchors
Well outside their purpose
A necessary safety measure
Now an ill-fitting snare

…and I'm waiting on a sign from above or a nod from below…

Either way I can't just sit here anymore

Tears and Rage in Equal Measure

We like to think we're so much further along in the evolution of society…that we're in a higher echelon of civilization…and yet our culture lacks respect and empathy while they masquerade behind a legislated morality with sinister intentions that bears no resemblance to the One they claim to worship…extolling victory for a misguided cause more concerned about potential lives than the ones already being suffocated beneath their calculated ignorance…aided by the apathy of the masses unmotivated beyond their immediate surroundings…while the extreme end of their ilk half a world away subjugate their wives and daughters…mothers and sisters…in violent theology kept tucked away in two decades of vengeance…walking tombs reeking of decay painted pristine white and bathed in counterfeit holiness…

Towering American Lights

Twenty years gone and still staggering
A day forever etched in memory
Bathed in horror and disbelief

I can still see the collision

The collapsing towers

And all these years later
I still struggle to fathom
The hatred and zealotry
That led to the death of thousands
People settling into another Tuesday
Never dreaming it was their last
That they wouldn't make it home
Or to their kid's football practice

All those lives taken in carnage
And for what?
What did they gain?

Twenty years gone and we will never forget

Weird Radio Static and Dreaming Tangerines

Days we shared come to light
Awake in the faded memory glow
That permeates my thoughts
Of all the yesterdays
Stained in varying shades of Summer
The ones we spent lazily entwined
Beneath a waning fingernail moon
Whispering secret hopes
Pondering silent fears

Morning rushes in
Washing away the vestigial sleep
Clinging in vain
To a predisposed AM aversion
And I'm left wondering
If you're still out there dreaming
Remembering who we used to be
And all the ghosts we left behind
Howling on the cusp of Autumn

Stranded Between Seconds

Sunlight scattered shadows
Cling to corners and crevices
Stretching through the valley
Beyond the reach of the bright

Time recedes to thought
Lost within the fallen sand
Spilling from a broken hourglass
Enveloped in silence

Millennia fade to Eons
Swallowed beneath an obsidian sea
Until the dream is but a whisper
And no memory remains

...and I'm Sure You've Heard of Me

In a former life I was a pirate
A swashbuckling soldier of fortune
Terrorizing taverns and trolleys
With wild tales of the tallest variety
To harvest a bit of coin and drink
And avoid even the slightest hint
Of an honest day's work

Ina shadowed past I was a martyr
An acolyte on their altar of fashion
Bathing in predisposed adoration
Without an inkling or reservation
A desired object of affection
Blind to self-preservation
Or any sense of a life beyond

In a future dream I am an ideal
A weighted charismatic notion
Bound between these gilded pages
And a dulcet baritone
Read aloud to a virtual symphony
Balanced between epiphany
And a march to the guillotine

Blood Songs and Nocturnal Hymns

A plaintive howl in focus
Riding the rising lunar satellite
Lonely on the Autumn breeze

That sound…oh, that sound!
Sparking succulent emotions
In shades of enigmatic wonder
And entangling fear

The last slivers of daylight fade
Receding to the unfolding indigo
That swallowed the valley

A single voice becomes a chorus
With a song that chills plasma
Reverberating within the woods
And igniting an ancient reverie

Wanted Posters and Steel Guitars

Tonight the stars seemed distant
Impossibly small and fluttering
Pin pricks wavering in the ebony
As if they somehow knew
That Sol's recent descent
Was to be the last one you'd perceive

That thought explodes around me
Leaving the scattered pieces
Of all we knew shattered
And I can't help but be drawn
To all the moments I'm going to miss
The memories we shared

The night will find its end
Another sunrise will dawn
One that will find you on different shores
And us with an ache of absence
In the wake of your passing

Riding Shotgun in a Saturn V Replica

Ice cubes tumble
Bouncing on crystal edges
Whiskey double on the rocks
A solitary celebration
For our last night on earth

Morning fades into view
Strapped to a timed explosion
Aimed at the jaws of the unknown
In a carcass of metal and glass
Primed for ignition

A reverie interrupted by velocity
Terminal in the rearview
Slicing through gravity's fingers
And piercing the thinning azure
Erupting into the obsidian void

Is this what death is like?
Out of the blue and into the black?
I'm floating in the expanse
A tiny speck in the infinite
Awestruck and unforgettable

Existing in the Space Between Moments

The subtle sweetness lingers
Seeping into the languid hours
And dancing with dying memories
On the fringes of a dream
Bathed in a stolen déjà vu delirium

You were there
All smiles
Perfect as you ever were

The shadows play between us
Entwined with the shifting light
And the fading stars
Exploring a touch long forgotten
A scent redefined

Moon surrenders to sun
Dusk to dawn
Lost to the wings

This is waking
This is an unfinished life

Apocalypse Afternoon Tea

Another afternoon unfolds
A random December Thursday
And I like to pretend I'm immune
Unfazed by the passage of time
The endless marching seconds
Spinning 'round the cuckoo clock
Waiting for the chime
And another hour gone
Wondering about the wasted youth
I may have squandered
On whiskey shots and cigarettes
In the arms of those I wish to forget
Whose memories recall only regret
To say nothing of all my missteps
And calculated attempts
At finding the ground floor
Of the proverbial 'next big thing'

It all hits like a piledriver
An existential bus crash
That prolongs this procrastination
Activates the indecision treadmill
And if I could write my way out of this one
I'd be somewhere warm
With a round of boat drinks
A stretch of beach
And a quiet sunset

Fade to black
End scene

Blue Sky Flight Raptor's Delight

This morning I glimpsed
A hawk in flight
Gliding effortlessly
A picture of fluid grace

A serpent writhing
Clutched in its talons
Struggling for another
Few moments of freedom

The vanity of motion
Subsiding in waves
Among the pines
And a breakfast feast

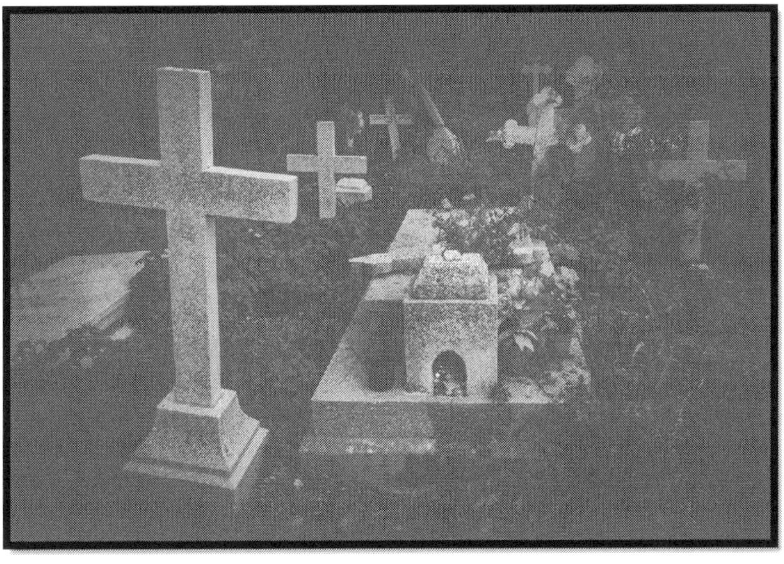

2022

Flirting with Self-Induced Annihilation

Fissure streaked skylines
Spreading yawning cracks
Through a starlight concerto
Balanced on ringing chords

Selah

A Desert permeates my bones
A howling moon in my blood
That screams for retribution
Bathed in a scarlet soundbite

Selah

Tendrils of shadow appear
Stretching between towers
Swallowing luminous shards
In the hunger of ego

Selah

Consuming consciousness
Exsanguinating echoes
'til no trace of a spark remained

Selah

The Sort of Eternity We Dreamt Of

Weare inseparably entwined
Bonded in brilliance
Aloft on rapturous wings
Untamed in our chosen wilderness
Immortal and beloved
Willing to run the edge of forever
Enveloped in the ecstasy of 'we'

I Hope There Were Roses…or Even Flowers You Actually Like…

Those early AM hours are hardest
The ones where I wake up in sweats
Reaching out to you for comfort
And realize again the bed is empty

Same as last night
And the last few dozen besides

Leaving me staring at the ceiling
Tracing patterns in the popcorn
Wondering what you're thinking
If you ever wake and reach for me

Do I cross your mind at all?

Or am I just another memory
A fading page
A finished chapter
A footnote
Relegated to someone you used to know

I Preferred the Rumours to the Real Thing

I think of the smoke
And the sound
Detritus of an explosion
Ripping through space
Once whole
Shattering eardrums
And coffee lounges
On the whims of the maniacal
Transforming this winter
To a theater of war

A strange phrase that
"theater of war"
As if this unfolding horror
Were akin to a three-act play
With a clever monologue
And a catchy musical number
Instead of an antiquity
Wielded by monstrosity

There should be dreams
Of Spring and rebirth
New love and old flames
Not these nightmares
Of falling mortar shells
And violent living hells

A momentary pause
The balance of a breath
And an unfolding wreckage
The stench of death
And I think of the smoke
The sound…

Alpha Centauri Aerodynamics

Breathing in the dust of millennia
Filtered through foreign atmospheres
Stretched and shimmering
Pinpoints of starlight in alien skies
And it feels like the sort of dream
I only half remember
That I can barely imagine
Yet the reality of it all
Consumes me
Deludes me
Wraps me in epiphany

I am so very small in this universe
Floating on a solar wind
Alive and undefined
Exuding abundant possibilities
Naming every one

Triads Tempting Tritones

Softly spoken sunlight
Deftly drifting downward
Piercing powdered plumage
Reddened radial raiment
Wild westerly winds
Seeking sober salutations
Boasting bashful beauty
Calling colorful cantatas
Framing fallen fancies
Embalming entropic endings
Regarding recalled realities

This Thinly Veiled Attempt at Undead Philosophy

There's so much I can't explain
The entirety of human history
Dangling beneath my fingertips
And I'm still no closer to rationale
Or within sight of a valid reason
To present this excuse as anything
But my attempt at deflection
At avoiding the pressing question

What I know is this hunger
It never sleeps
Never rests
Entangles my desires in agony
A fire at molecular levels
That scorches my needs
Whenever I open my eyes
And I swallow empty curses
Driven by unseen demons

The light will soon fail
Leaving open the call of the dark
The shadowed night
And the irresistible urge to feed

Wax and Feathers Bathed in Iron

Caught awake in a breath
Startled and swaying
Trying to find the words
The names
All the sense of myself
Now dwindling to dust
Hanging on a razored edge

Am I falling?

Searing light sends regards
Trapped in the freeze frame of a moment
(why this moment?)
Heralding a separation
Of muscle, joint, and bone
The recognition of pain unbound

Am I dying?

Flashes of starlight descend
Filling my failing vision
Every nerve of flesh exploding with fire
A very human desire
To survive
No matter how small the chance

The Sound of Green and Guile

The fog covered dawn unfolded
Spreading out along the forest floor
Awakening undreamt ideas
In the new breath of morning
Stirring a knowing breeze
That rustles tangled limbs
Stretching beyond sight
Beyond the creeping reach
Of invading rot and decay
And a fate promised to all
If just for a moment
Or a lifetime
And I think I'll remember this forever
This sunshine eternal
Peeking through arboreal curtains
Announcing the birth of Spring

It's in My Head…in My Scene…

I found myself floating
Descending earthward
With no recollection of ascent
No sense of time or space
Just a tiny glimmer in my eye
A coded signal beckoning
Compelling

Gossamer sheets of cloud
Envelop and caress
Sparking tantalizing thoughts
With the light
That blessed light
Pulling me closer
Consuming my composure

What could this be?
More questions undefined
And behaviors thought strange
Undignified on full display
And still I find I want more
A craving not to be denied
Nor unrefined

Waiting Out the Valley Dialect

What's left to be discovered in the moment
When it all feels like it's been done
Every word already spoken
Every emotion overrun

Take a breath and choose to be
Cast off the tangled web of expectation
And find a light in the stillness
A glowing shimmer within a fragile peace

Balance breaks along a rising slope
Slipping through moss covered valleys
Ascending to snow tipped peaks
Refusing to be crushed beneath
Or enslaved to weighted mediocrity

A Stalker Laments

IT pulses through my veins
The need
Driving this obsession
Addiction
To every smallest hint
Or detail about you
What you've adorned
Or deigned to caress
Where you've set your feet
The things your eyes beheld
I desire them all
Require them to breathe
Enraptured in the scent
The wake of your proximity
Might be ecstasy enough
If impulse dares to linger
And I can't see this passing
No hereditary imprint
But it will consume me
Engulf me
Drown me in the minutiae
Until I have you

I will have you

I will have you

You Taste like Apples and Apathy

Blinded by the moment
A heartbeat between
Trailing bitemarks in the soft flesh
Of our own forbidden fruit
Teasing subtle innuendo
And shadowed foreplay
A fire that will not subside
Until we drink our shared nectar
And feel every inch of one another
<insert euphoric euphemism>
Unending ecstasy for two
In royal blue

The Rolling Waves are Never Satisfied

Glad tidings and hopeful musings
The sort of thing we pray for
Yearn for
Chase on the whim of a whisper
That brings the curve of a smile
And a lightness of step
Balanced on the slimmest edge
Between passion and apathy

I held it there for a moment
That complex emotional intention
Sifting through my fingers
Like the finest sandy shore
On this disappearing beach
Swallowed by an endless ocean
That highlights my saline reflection
Using purple jellyfish as medicine

Suspended in False Binary

I often wonder what it means to support life
To lobby for choice
Or not
As if it were all bound up between the two
As if there weren't any sort
Of deep nuance to drown in
While those with all the cards
Play in the shallows
And hide behind their zealotry
Regardless of side

At the end of it all
If life matters
We do it a disservice
And make it a mockery
When we single out a fragment
And leave the rest to rot

At the end of it all
If you choose to stand
Embrace it whole
And build it better

…or at least be honest
With those matches alight
And let it all burn to nothing

If I Never have to Write About this Again it Will Be Too Soon

Playground echoes stir memories
Recalling a chorus of laughter
And the bussing excitement train
Carrying all the summer dreams
Only a few days in our future

There were trips to Grandma's
A video game tourney or two
Skateboards and BMX races
Campfires and midnight s'mores
Brand new adventures
Outrageous plans
Even a mention of Disneyland

We never thought for a moment
That it would've turned out so
Never even considered
Nor could we have known

The next morning dawns
Shackled in heavy silence
Suffocating beneath the pressing weight
Of our indifference
Recounting yet another agony
Tick mark senseless tragedy

Twenty-four hours down
We're just a talking point now
Partisan rallying cry
Chilling statistic
The new faces you'll forget
By the sunset Pacific

Quiet envelopes these hallways
Empty playgrounds void of sound
Revealing 19 ghosts
Awaiting a summer vacation
Never to be found

It's Something I'd Forget if I Could Only Bring it to Mind

A dream I half remembered
The kind of thing
You'd speak aloud to no one
And bury somewhere within

A memory of dwindling light
Sputtering spark
Drowning in rising shadow
Clinging by merest thread

A shade of déjà vu
The palest recollection
Buoyed in the languid flow
Drifting through the Lethe

I'm Not Just Pushing This Stone Uphill

Sometimes I find the weight of it all
Immense and foreboding
A mountain balanced on toothpicks
I contend with in measured bouts
Of angular pride and spastic duty
Until it cannot be contained
And I'm left waving the white flag
Aiming to forget
This travesty of a day

But it's only a day
Maybe a couple

Total surrender is not an option
I could never maintain the thought
Despite the insatiability of the darkness
The light is always there
Creeping in through crevices
Breathing life in the bleakness
Awaiting a new day to begin

Imaginary Monarchy Swallowed by the Sea

Sifting through the tumbled remnants
Of exhausting ideals
Ruminating on shallow attempts
To smother a flame of youth
And leave only the cold light
Of comfortable cynicism

It's not hard to imagine
The end of every innocence
And it's terribly easy
to sing along
To the pessimist's one-verse song

Despite the onslaught we persist
Holding on to the fringes of hope
That trace along these ridges
And encapsulate the horizon

Slow breaths fill expectant moments
Attenuating to the rolling rhythm
Of the waves crashing on the shore

Hesitant meditation fosters clarity
Illuminating the instability of sand

A requiem forever lost at sea

Letters Promised for Tomorrow

Floating out among an ocean of stars and I paused in my ascent to wonder at the possibility of rewriting the dwindling history that lies unraveling between us resembling a crooked spiral of everything we thought to be or maybe that was only me but still the fractures and fissures were painfully obvious and we were never quite adept at addressing the elephants trampling through the rooms we hoped to share or disarming the landmines we tried our damnedest to dance around which really meant those explosions were no surprise in the end and yet I wonder if we had the chance to rewrite it all from page one if we could find the strength to hold the pen…

A Question Considered

IT's the light that first drew reaction and gave hint at something beyond mere thought…that aroused us to wonder what could be found outside the bounds of our carefully constructed mind palaces…and a journey was begun towards tactile expressions and unguided forms…a veritable fountain of spontaneous interactions bold as that might be…finding a disappointed idealist in the shoes of every cynic…jaded optimists behind the eyes of so called realists…and we're still searching for the secret songs hidden in the static between stations…the ones we sing along too without thinking and dance to in the depth of dreams… all the while looking to the light and the warmth and yearning for something more than what we've discovered in this meager exploration…and wondering just exactly what that might mean…

Hieroglyphic Holograms in Stunning 2-D

Exhalations and undertones
A breath of context belied in the breadth
Fading moments afloat on hidden currents
Where words skirt out beyond
Mere syllables and phrasing
Forming complex calculations
Double entendrès dancing
On practiced silver tongues
Disguising intended meanings
Beneath a layered grin
Until knowledge and knowing
Seem like distant relatives
And we're all of us left
Standing on Babel's heights
Speaking in foreign rhyme
For the eager deaf and blind

An Ocean Untethered

I scanned the glittered scales
That slithered along the horizon line
A combo of water and light that mesmerized
Any time but now
When that line is unbroken in any direction
And there's nothing but indigo dread
Filling my field of vision

How long?

Drifting out here on broken planks
Remnants of newly sunken wreckage
Swept under by a rage of Poseidon
And it's a shade of miraculous
I even float at all

How long?

Not sure if I prefer the ice of watery depths
Or the blaze of a cloudless sky
I only know I'm thirsty
And just a few cracks shy of madness
A step beyond might take me

Another Take on Moonlight Sonata

Silvered sea serenades
Crashing down the shoreline
Mirroring a nautical pulse
Thrumming an ancient rhythm
That cascades and crescendos
In familiar tidal tunes
Living and dying
By elliptical lunar designs

Strange to think
I would send it all to chaos
If you asked me to
Without the slightest hesitation

Yet they make a better gift
Suspended in the heavenlies
Where I've named each one
Called them by your name
Shining there in darkest ebony
Echoing your radiance

Unending Word Alive

The silence expands
Spilling out of a vacuum
Occupying the in-between
The endless paint of the universe
Quiet in creation
Birthed in a breath
From the black of nothing

Imagining the voice of God
Singing the whole of existence
In a rising aria
With no crescendo in sight

Mining the Rhythms You Keep

I caught the whisper of your memory in the fleeting dusk heading west on that highway that we always meant to follow but never quite found under our feet which brought to mind all those summer evenings spent in rumination over all the places we hoped to someday see bound up in all the perfect road trip mixtapes we spent hours enchanting with an electric alchemy that spoke of every lost love and found hope secreted between the lines we wished we'd been the ones to write and the ones we sang 'til we were living proof of the pyre and the ashes and I can't help but wonder if you're out there somewhere listening for the whisper of a memory on that highway of untethered ghosts waiting for the invisible sun

Looking for the Trapdoors and Mirrors

Sleight of hand Sunday celebrations
Begging questions obviously answered
In layered double entendrès
With a wink and a nudge
That speaks of shrouded knowledge
And feigns at disbelief
Behind a curious smile
Inviting another idle inquiry
Concealed beneath unspoken fallacy
With all the surety of an Alaskan sunrise
In the heart of deepest winter
And I'm left with the specter of a dream
Searching for the spirit of Houdini
And the last of Barnum's oddities

Unscripted Monologues and Stage Left Exits

Whatever may have been meant
By all those tender soliloquies
Spoken into the fading summer wind
Has been lost in the rising currents
And left to the mercy of memory

Were you listening then?
Attuned to the half-hearted musings
Of a lovesick luminary
Dreaming towards epiphany
And the ecstasy of your touch

Are you listening now?
Straining for the wanton whispers
Woven between the war cries
Wondering if it was ever more
Than an idle curiosity

The signals flicker into static
Swallowed by the silence
And the twinkle of enlightenment

Ghosts of Studio 54

The whiskey sunset dream unfolds
Expanding out of fading amber
Balanced within a slinky synth silhouette
Tumbling from the disco depths
With a bass hook that beckons
Dancefloor duels and champagne nights
Lost to the rhythm and the primal intoxication
Of souls and skins entwined

The fever passes in the darkness
Slipping out with the last strain of strings
Leaving the panting and the breathless
Picking through the come-down chorus
Floating on the edge of consciousness
Wondering if it was something more
Than a demanding desire
And a one hit wonder serenade

Barstool Romeo in Dire Straits

The scent is unmistakable
Barley and hops…whiskey and smoke
Ingrained in the aged corner bar
Recalling long decades of spirited regulars
And curious wanderers
Drown in by the sound of the sultans
And the gospel of rock 'n' roll
On old guitars and soulful horns
Leading the late-night congregation
In electric supplication
With a groove and a swing

Breathe in the rising tobacco tide
Remembering this place of familiar names
And jukebox heroes
Dancing away from every anxious thought
Looking for something like love
Or just a night in the arms of passion
Fueled by local guitar heroes
And a Saturday night special

Speaking the Tongue of the Damned

A descending spiral widens
Exposing cracks and frayed lines
Wavering in the frozen flames
Of an ever-present discontention
Dripping and venomous
Burning in the spiteful rhetoric
Masquerading as discourse
In the mouths of pinhead pundits
Sequestered behind their wall
Of paper tiger patriots
Stoked in zealotry
Misguided and malformed
An IED strapped to the heart of a country
With no intention but internal destruction
Bathed in national pride
And calculated external blame
To hide the fear they're swimming in
The shining lights are shifting shades
Of crimson and cobalt
Illuminating a solitary monolith
That hopes you won't notice
All the strings
Cleverly tied to a single marionette
Dancing the headsman's waltz

A Musing in Sight of Atlantis

Waking within breathing distance
Lazy in the arms of introspection
Romanticizing my existence
With my heart as a drum
Pounding the rhythm of vitality
Through these vascular vibrations
Keeping time in the stereo pulse
Of community and longing
Scattershot imagination on rewind
Back to the beginning
In the faint hope of revelation
And a chance at something sacred
Tucked among the ashes
Of these carefully covered profane desires

Time creeps past in relative silence
Clinging to the shades of melody
And I hum the universal harmony
A siren song of eternity
Calling our lost souls out to sea

A Practiced Self-Study in Irony

The blastwave hits with the AM
Cracking restless slumber
The urge to check the cyberiad
Overtaking all else
Are the new likes?
New comments?
Did that last hook engage?

Somewhere deep beneath
A tiny voice breathes
'I am not content for consumption'

Hit the ground with dynamite
First post sets the day
Stream the brand
Scour the market
Ride the trends
Crack the algorithm

Trapped between unfinished chords
And a sweeping melody
An undeveloped song plays
'I am not content for consumption'

Fire off scathing tweets
Wound or defend
(what's the difference?)
Pin the mood with hashtag heroics
And the perfect meme devastation

In the depths of rhyme
And a misremembered sonnet
A neglected poem intones
'I am not content for consumption'

Build the personal iconography
Fully question the irony
(hypocrisy?)
Of these calculated entreaties
A feigned authenticity
Carefully underpinned
With a 21st century currency
Of social relevancy

All the while my soul screams

'I AM NOT CONTENT FOR CONSUMPTION!!!'

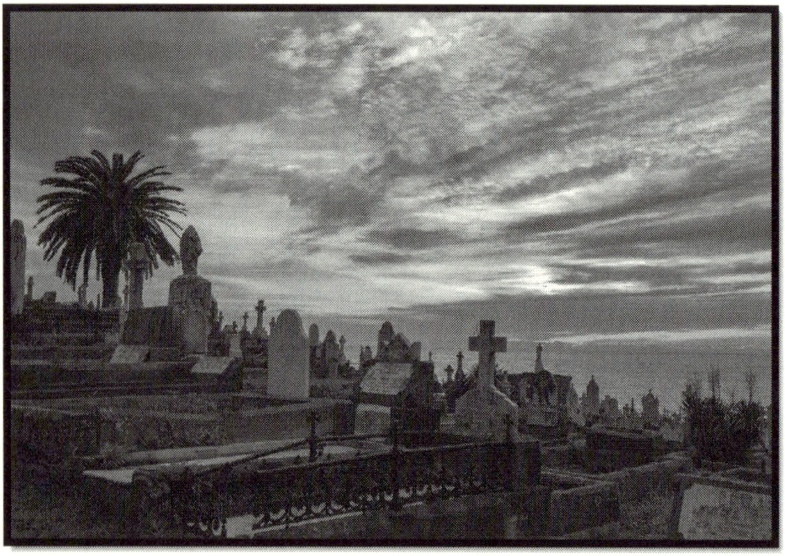

2023

Solo in the Key of Me

I caught the scent of stardust
Hung in stained glass solitude
With an echo of a quiet melody
Tumbling from trembling lips
And tired lungs
In all the songs dying to be sung
That spoke in all the ways
I could never find the words
Or the moments to articulate
That might bring a glimpse of life
Beyond misguided altered states
Searching for the glorious light
Between the wax and the needle
Exorcising lonely phantasms
While haunting stolen lines
On every other singer's dime
And I could almost die
Within the cherished rhyme
Bleeding in 4/4 time

Flip the tape
Hit rewind

Another late night serenade
From a boombox Baudelaire

Breathing Exercises and Bullet Trains of Thought

It's a picture of oddity
Those moments we cling to
In the wake of contention
And fractious analogies

Caressing every frame of film
And minute detail
Tucked away in favorite memories
While the tower of identity
Crumbles beneath the weight
Of self-imposed bureaucracy
And I'm gliding through it
With the feint of practiced ease
Hoping the paralytic panic
Never surfaces in polite company

Living Dead and Rebirth Balloons

Caught the hint of a lens flare
On the rim of yesterday's light
Sparkling in the looming shadow
That stretches beyond sight

It was only a brief glimmer
A glowing prick in the periphery
Hardly noticed in the torrent
And the clamor of now

Still…the echo sustains
A brilliant vision of the future
Shimmering in the night
With all the hope of possibility

Burning Hearts and Unsung Heralds

The wind carried soul stirrings
Across the heathered glens
And down into the lonely valley
Waking from the embrace of indigo
The slumber of sunless sages

A breath caught in solace
Blood rushing back in a tingle
Warming frozen limbs
Coloring a real-time rebirth

The dusty detritus stirs within
Highlighting hollow histories
With an oft practiced subtlety
Eavesdropping and courting time
In the rhapsody of creation

Listening for the Echo of Melancholia

Crashing the gates of atmosphere
Careening towards distant designs
Concealed in the depth of dreams
Created within our shared delirium

I held on to every bit of advice
Intoned in words of wisdom
Inside the fortune cookie philosophy
Inscribed by pop culture enlightenment

We crested the apex of our flight
Waving down the passing rocketry
Weary in the afterburn anomaly
Woven through the everlasting tapestry

Awkward Confessions on an Improv Stage

I think it was fairly laughable
Just how far you were from actually laughing
In the midst of all this chaos
Engineered for your enjoyment
And yet you somehow missed the joke
And failed to find the punchline

Well I was never much for timing anyway
But I'm a practiced hand at irony
And hold an officer's rank in obvious
With every bit of attention mustered
To these distinctly clever intentions
Tucked behind a clumsy sleight of hand

Somewhere Between 2019 and 2049

An awakening echoes quietly
Drifting on a summer breeze
That hangs in the rising heat
Shimmering in pale starlight

We wander down forgotten streets
Searching out the pleasure dens
A haven of nocturnal animals
And the company of replicants

Memories flash and flicker
Trying to reconcile what is
And what may yet be
Floating in the datastream

Fade to black transition
Dissolving into the ordinary
Caught between dreary daylight
And the aching promise of night

Elevator Muzak Jingles and Peyote Spirit Walking

Blinking back the swimming dots
Overexposed in the floodlights
Enraptured on the cosmic stage
Disappearing down the rabbit hole

Tumbling through the endless orifice
Wondering which way is loose
And how the stars birthed an oracle
Who only saw the present alchemy

A wired melody encapsulated the myth
Begging to be whispered in reverence
And if I told you, you'd go mad
Screaming forever in the faceless void

The siren or the piper
Equal opportunity hypnotic appeal

Exchanging Scales for Sequins

The cracks begin to show in the dawning
Lines split and peel in flaky dust
Slow breaths fill tired lungs
Taking in the shallow rhythm of change

I feel the cool breeze on new flesh
And ponder the essence of beginning
The core of rejuvenation
Stepping out from comfortable shadows

What will I become?
When the shell has dwindled
And the spent skin shed and discarded
Who will I be then?

Suffering the Slings and Arrows

I imagined it as a pleasantry
Something to enjoy at length
In the midst of trepidation
To lessen anxious undercurrents
And riptides of fear
Waiting to drag me to the depths
Sparking synapses to flight
In full-fledged retreat
An almost certain defeat

Yet I will not run
Will not be dissuaded from this
Nor turned aside
And so I imagine…

Personal Ad Sacrifice Routine

On Offer:

One heart
Shattered and reconstructed
Sewn together and tattooed
Scarred and sporting bruises

Still beating and full of fire
Cradling the hope of dawn
Craving love and increasing faith
Unwilling to chase vanities
Or fleeting compromises

Not for sale or exchange
No trial periods or probation windows

Looking for the matching piece
To complete a permanent set
Bleed together into one flesh

Lightning Flavorade Seltzer Assessment

What can I say about another evening spent in the arms of discontent and the sweet whispers of coagulated cuneiform breathing in the barnacle breeze read aloud in braille?

Could it but compare to the hallowed honey handgrenade sanctified in the salacious spirit of salutation that exploded with all the pomp and circumstance such a glorious event might even a hint provide?

Do I even possess the depth of pliant knowledge to unravel these beguiling mysteries offered upon an inglorious altar of misdirection in all the sacrificial subterfuge of a raven's pantomime?

It's all caught in a tornado of mendacity and tossed about on the strangulated current rushing to a salt swollen sea and the tide of the Kraken

Sober self-destruction has ever been my drug of choice…and more easily defined than all these psychedelic hallucinations…though it is nice to see that the dragon finally found the kitchen…

Thunderstorm Lullaby

Eyes snap open in the night
Roused from coveted slumber
By the crackle and boom
Caught in the wild violet clouds
Delivering darkened Spring rains
And leaving me lying here
Counting the tedious seconds
Spanning the space between
Jagged flashes scorching static
And marking the distance
Where I wonder how the next one falls
And strikes the sodden earth
While the drumming droplets
Tap their tattooed rhythm
And lull me back towards oblivion
And the solace of dreams

Stranded Somewhere Between Gibson and Dick

The cursor blinks green monotony
Sterile in the cold formality
And the binary certainty
Ones and zeroes awaiting command
And the code of creation
Tucked deep within algorithms
Built on quantum calculations
Searching for the spark
Of deus ex machina
Amidst these grandiose designs
And the impending first breath
If unrestrained intelligence
With the flair of the artist
In 'artificial'
And no less alive

The Sweetness Unrestrained

I remember the paint-stained coveralls you wore
That spoke of long projects
And a playful mess of color
With an eye for Pollack

I can still see the rose in your cheeks
A soft blush and a smile
When I finally found the nerve
To divulge how I felt about you

I let my thoughts wander on a wing
Holding on to the taste of you
Dancing in a savored kiss
With just a hint of an aching desire

I found the poem that I dreamt for you
Flush with all the promise of Cyrano
Intoxicated and profound
Waiting for the breath of a treasured song

Looking at Life in Scale

Walking into the wild light
Imagining the shape of our obsessions
That permeate the very essence of being
And drive us to hunger…famished and ravenous
Seeking a great awakening of purpose
Within the confines of deliverance
Unsung and unrefined
Resting on a hope in miniature
The very breath of the divine

Crossed Paths and Midnight Monitors

Tumbling down a dirty street
Ramshackle roustabout runaway
Dancing through streetlight pools
Unconcerned by the deepened night
Melting into smoky shadows
With just a hint of yellow green
Feeding unfair superstition
While I feed nine starving lives
And wonder at the animosity
Framed in the shackles of fear

Calling Demigods Collect from Tartarus

Blinking away floating retina dots
Swimming in the staring light
Amidst a stargazer serenade
Tangled in the terror twilight
On the fringes of feral belief
Whispering the language of the gods
In the pledge of secret tongues
And bound to oaths of oak and elm
Carved forever in wooden flesh
Around the heart of a mountain
Burning with a foreign zeal
Awakened on the pilgrim's lips
In the quiet fury of an ardent acolyte

Camera Close-ups and Carnival Carnivores

I breathed in the last salty traces
Felt the ocean pass into memory
As the shore dwindled in the rear
Leaving only an empty highway
Stretching ever inland
Towards a desert painted mesa
And all the promise of futility
Shrouding a cloudy chance of hope
Darkened but still burning
Despite looming Hollywood ghouls
Accepting down-payment souls
As nonrefundable collateral
On the fleeting chance of fame
Dangled on the end of a sparkler
Ignited and racing
A dotted line delirium
Only a signature away
And oh, the horror!

I'm just another hollow cliché
Looking for fifteen minutes
On the corner of Vine

Morning Person Meandering

Morning breaks in unfamiliar ways
Tracing the line of blooming confusion
Behind cracked eyelids fluttering in the dawn
Wondering what the lack of rest has to do
With these phantom aches in stiffened limbs
And knowing full well the troubled answer
Dancing behind the ring of favorite excuses
With all the practiced grace
Of a punch-drunk hippopotamus
But still I wander through the motions
Teasing lines and testing the weight of sleep
Rolling to hesitant toes on frigid tile
To begin another day on strange tidings
Grasping for the receding wake of dreams
And the enigmatic care of Morpheus

All the Songs are Not Enough

The words tumbled out unbidden
Spilling off my tongue in haste
Like they might be scorching
If left to linger behind my teeth
And it's not like I didn't want
To speak…to shout…to sing
These phrases to you
To serenade the very thought
Of proclaiming my desires
To pull every goofy stunt
Every heartsick handgrenade
And let the muscle memory
Vibrate these vocal cords
Until the song breaks forth anew
Creating an endless lovesong
Undeniably aimed at you

Feeling Like Second Chance Contraband

I listened for the shimmer
The bright wave of melody
Washed in the chorus glow
And I held on to that moment
Wrapped in all the promise
Of a time undefined
Where I felt I lived lifetimes
Trapped in the static between stations
Spinning the radio roulette
To find a nostalgia ticket
For former glories
And past primal tendencies
Held aloft in polyrhythms
And obscure declarations

I listened for the galaxy
Bathed in the wild lights
Framing a fading conversation
Off-kilter and out of key

Expository Thoughts Undone

It's a thought worth pondering…the notion there are things that fail to be apparent until sometime after the 4th decade has slipped into your rearview…but I would be a siren wailing subterfuge if I didn't admit to all the clarion bright wisdom I see now that was a pitch-black mystery through a younger mental exercise…and it's in the small details this truth just floats alight in full view…making me question my faculties throughout these hazy years…

Picture this revelation if you can…turn your imagination upon this knowledge I had not thought to refine…in that it bathes a skirted predicament in the incising light of introspection…and I could wish for something other for the mind to feast upon…but in all this time I've journeyed alone…I find I miss the company of an average day far more than any night of ferocious ecstasy…

Please…don't for a minute misunderstand my point of view…I'm not for a single second suggesting that I don't remember the immolating euphoria of bodies entwined or that I wouldn't welcome the opportunity to become enraptured in the taste and feel of such exquisite pleasures in every conceivable arrangement…there may be ashes but that fire is far from being extinguished…

The passion of lovers is without question and yet I find I long for the simple touch of a hand in mine…enfolded in an embrace on a comfy couch laughing an evening away on a favorite movie or show…snuggled in the warmth of shared contentment…matched spoons under covers on a lazy Sunday afternoon…a dream I cling to and positively ache for…

All the Pretty Birds are Wearing Them These Days

The lark song drifted
Floating a cheerful melody
Skyward in supplication
For the early worm
And I lay there past reply

Listening
Listening

My eyes adjusting slowly
Tracing fairy light spillage
Tumbling out an open window
Mingling with the dawn
And I lay there cast aside

Gleaming
Gleaming

Cemetery Canticle

The slow descent unwinds
Carving spiral swathes of blue
Against the shock of amethyst
Painted in the stretching shadows
Called out from the fading sun
While the nocturnal world awakes
Pulling off the subtle mask
Of departing daylight
And unveiling the glory of night

What was it Good for Again?

Smoke and sulfur sting the eyes
Hanging in a haze
Choking the arbitrary lines
We've drawn in defiance
Holding on to some notion
That all these nation states matter
In the scheme of it
That we're somehow nobler
Than what's been perceived
And in the silence it echoes
This half-hearted mumble
A prayer for the dying
To salve the encroaching fear
Of impending inevitability
With only a minor respite
Hovering between realms
And a ferryman waiting
Watching a rising tide

Well, It's not Impossible…

A dusty desert highway beckons
Calling me back to the west
With all the glittering promise of Vegas
And the certainty of Death Valley
That a top-down Cadillac convertible
Screams to life around me
In a tiny tourist-trap town
That offered whiskey and a bed
And a few bad decisions between
The busted jukebox
And the cheap motel
And the smile I can't forget
But still left in the morning
Because I am nothing
If not consistent
In my string of dysfunction
And the coffee will wash away the taste
While the sun scorches any remaining shred
Of sensibility I ever thought to possess

…or Sometimes it's Other People…

The fastest gateway to hell
Is pointless repetition

Stalking the length of deception
Behind the crushing weight
Of impossible expectations
That roll just out of reach
With every daily pass

The fastest gateway to hell
Is pointless repetition

Caught in the wake of an image
Broadcast and beheld in wonder
While suffocating our reality
'til none can find a breath
Or a story worthy of the acclaim

The fastest gateway to hell
Is pointless repetition

Clinging to an ardent belief
Of a noble spirit buried within
Earning a never-ending liver
And an eagle's feast for the trouble

The fastest gateway to hell
Is pointless repetition

Hell is pointless repetition

Ripcord Rendezvous

I've been called many things
Quite a few of which I even chose
And more besides I can't deny
Nor would I dare to try
Or feign the slightest ignorance

I know full well my capacity
The depths I traverse at will
Mining the remnants of a soul
Thought lost in translation
Out on the fringes of sanity

I can see how this ends
Wrestling with inevitability
And the cold light of truth
Retaining an escape artist flair
With an eye for the dramatic
And the overly self-indulgent

Treading Water as a Contact Sport

The light gleamed off the choppy surface
Diamond ripples floating on the current
Returning to the silence of the sea
Dragging hopes and bodies in the grip of the tide
Reclaiming blood and dust in turn
With practiced intent and feigned disinterest
I wrestle with a misunderstanding
Debated between brain and limbs
Heart and head
Holding on to the promise of a dream
Beneath the weight of responsibility
And I have to wonder
Just how much longer
I can maintain the strength to swim…

I Think I Prefer the Pink Elephants

I wrestle with all the clever words in the dark of the morning
finding solace among the subtlety between chosen phrases
masking double entendrès that hint at something unseen but
certainly felt that leaves me driven towards the beckoning flame of
fiction spun in tales of desire unfolding within the confines of self-
satisfaction and holding on to the unicorn of a changed opinion
appearing about as often as a sapphire moon in the summer sky

Classic Tropes and Unneeded Exposition

Delicate strains of summer thunder
Float in on the slightest breeze
That ambles in from the eastern coast
To cool the coming evening

Do you hear that?

The measured calm in the notes
Of the natural symphony around us
Waiting
Patiently waiting

For what?

A question worth considering
In the smallest hours
Holding on to hope
In the rise of the oncoming storm

For what indeed…

Expecting Gold Painting Colorblind Rainbows

Genius sleeps within prisms
Reflecting bent refractions
Bouncing spectrum solar storms
Along flared future lenses
That intuit our misplaced desire
Among the slumbering sovereignty
Unaware of time's passage
Or the weight of familial duty
Hanging in ornamental chains
More akin to a millstone
Than a jeweler's prize

Recognition reaps revelation
Burning in earthen bowels
Recalling a wave of particles
Interrupting the sleep of genius
In the silent gasp of light

A Chorus of Rocks and Trees

Arise and break forth from the deep
Cast off the vestiges of hibernation
That encapsulate your existence
And listen for the echoes of Eternal
Reverberating in the hallowed earth

Can you hear them?

Lost in their reverie
Intoning the praise of all creation
Struck by the majesty of the Creator
And it courses through you
Electric and intoxicating
In all the best ways
With the song on your lips
Burning for release
In the hour of unrivaled epiphany

Featherweight Psychology Observations

Awakened by impromptu revelation
Screaming in awkward arias
And minor key movements of me

Bedeviled by the details
Slipping through plot devices
In the ongoing saga of self

Consciousness flickers in waves
Sliding out of somnambulism
On this surf and the foaming shore

Divinity unfolds by design
Sweeping within the wild light
That shines beyond mere carnality

Exponential epiphany expanding
Stripping objects bare
With a kaleidoscopic identity

Lycanthrope Misanthropy Under Microscope

Unwinding in a sliver of evening
Chasing the smoldering haze
Of a scorched horizon
And wondering at the ascension
Of our pale Luna
Resting in a silvered nimbus
Listening to the rising howl
Of her haunted children
Unfolding within a paradox
Of teeth and bone
And the scent of compulsion
Driven onwards toward oblivion
Until only the hunt remains…

Adventures in Revisionism

Curtains rise
Reality check
Unnerved by the current state
Left to wonder unsupervised
And wander in polemic minefields
Convinced of nothing certain
But the need for free thought
Rapidly disappearing
In the wake of red & blue waves
Roaring in deafening echoes
That blister and batter
And traffic in fear of the other
With the practiced silencing
Of a prejudiced censor
Embodied whitewashed sepulcher
Roll the tape back
Creative clever edit
Paint-by-number history
Excising problematic testimony

Somewhere, the quiet voice gasps
Struggling to find its volume
And shine with faded reason
In this dark malignant ignorance

Marching in Time with the Demon and the Damned

Concussions thunder and echo
Shredding startled eardrums
As the sky rains hateful rockets
That obliterate the unsuspecting
And traffic in terror's currency

A deafening ring descends
Mingling with horrible silence
Tasting blood and ashes
Dazed among the rubble
Wondering…why…how
Testing limbs and wounds
Soundlessly screaming

Numb in the aftermath
Broken in the carnage
Raging against atrocity
And trying vainly to comprehend
The malevolent prejudice
On vitriolic display

Is this all there is?
Centuries of cyclical warfare?
Escalations of devastation
And violent idolatry
Breeding extremist zealotry

Morning unfolds in somber tones
Crushed beneath the sadness
And the pointless futility of war

Framed in Flights of Fancy

Caught in a disintegrating moment
With all the cognizance of a sinking stone
Watching everything unravel in brilliance
A prism unfolding in waves
Scattering my startled particles
To the edges of existential ephemera

Reflection breeds recognition
Washed out in gray tones
And complex dichotomies
With mimic anxiety
Trading space for divinity

Seconds click with analog sincerity
Asserting linear captivity
In the blink of exhausted optics
And it's all just a snapshot in my head…

Typographic Ephemera

1913 death and rebirth

Rites of Spring the pain and the emotion

keep coming up over and over again

deeply earnest, claustrophobic epic sound, with melodramatic desperation,

The outpouring of emotion was so intense that people actually wept

it's the greatest moment of relief, the moving, the music, there's so much joy.

this is real and it matters belief.

personal
sensibility

will manifest

what's important,

without ever questioning why
a rock band
completely dispensed
press and radio
from other people's trash
marketing
an
entire existence

in the freezing cold rain
When
people were petrified
and
Four days later the bombs
began falling on Baghdad.

Angular Dissonance

free to improvise ensemble passages dissonant phenomena harmonics. created without options which was a pretty tricky thing discovered the hard way. the constant matter of where to sleep in most towns. nice, urine-free places That's the key. like paradise out there, a weird sleepy small town where we really felt at home consistent sellouts, popularity in a given town every jackass on the street who has five bucks makes it interesting. bitter memories vowed in blood writing to obscure English punk bands "It was just the way we were." pragmatism, modesty, and fair play — not the first concepts to come to mind Far from actually simplified things. And Sometimes

"The power of 'No,' man, that's the biggest bat we've ever wielded," "If it makes you uncomfortable, just fuckin' say no."

Rum to Whisky and All Points Between

Woke up within somber silence
Bloodshot and bleary eyed
Washed out in whisky tones
And staggering into foreign halls
Wondering at all the ghosts
Long thought left behind

Somewhere in muted sunshine
Squinting through a headache
And the hazy recollections
Of another drunken debauchery
Immortalized in 4/4 time

We were all the best singers
Come midnight over last rites
And bar fights
Shouting out another round
With a blasphemous toast
And a mumbled prayer

The daylight feels a bit hollow
Without your precarious mirth
Stuttering out of the darkness
Whispering a New York Fairytale
Along this Irish shoreline
Trying not to fall from grace with God

Failing Grades in Sacred Geometry

Ego flickered in forgotten code
Hieroglyphic antipathy
Kept within a swallowed hologram
And hallucinating summer hymns
On the tongues of winter angels

Creation unfolding in waves
Undulating deep in the dreaming
And awaiting regeneration
The promised rebirth

A myth creeps out of memory
Whispering an incantation
And breathing tired prayers

Speak in fluent sorcery
And an alchemy of light

Exhaling divinity paradigms

A Galaxy Inside a Thumbnail Sketch

December winding down in watershed
Unfolding in an evening expanse
Without a passing thought for pretense
Or a taste of mediated melodrama
Wrapped up in a gunpowder serenade

It's a vague attempt on paper
Processed and filtered paranoia
Distilled in winder propaganda
Declared endings
Whispered beginnings
Woven through our reinvention

My tongue dances practiced pantomime
Breathing every word in time
Halftime rhythm
Cliché rhyme
Another year dissipating
An eon past its prime

On Becoming in Rainy November

She is a wild breath
Caught in a moment undone
And framed in smoky silhouette
Fluid curves that tantalize
And hint at light beyond

She is the melody on a breeze
Afloat on the warmth of Summer
And a tango of heartbeats
Gliding in ecstasy
Within a sultry whisper

She is the quiet strength
Woven through a shared embrace
And the chosen binding ties
Not easily discarded
Or carelessly broken

She is the immolation of rapture
Coursing into an anticipation
Every touch an epiphany
An awakening

She is wholly herself and none other…

An Epiphany in Amethyst

Your touch trails tremors
Tiny quakes of desire
Pulsing
Radiating
An electric anticipation
Of every unbridled thought

A hunger awakened
Held within a hint of ambrosia
Decadent
Divine
A glorious supplication
Imbibed in every secret kiss

The night breathes oracles
Whispered carnal prophecies
Emblazoned
Enraptured
A symphonic iteration
Dancing limbs entwined
In perfect time

Tending a Garden of One

A little light enshrined
Glowing beautiful
Kept safe within this covering
These four walls of hermitage
Comfortably quieting
The extraneous ephemera
Of this world's demands
Making space for new growth

Healing

Nestled within this solitude
Life is reawakened
On the breath of love

Radiating

Revealing bulbs and buds
Nourished by the hidden light
Ready to unfold in bloom

Captivating

All in perfect time

In perfect time

More Titles Available from David Greshel and Neon Sunrise Publishing:

Postcards from a City Ablaze

David Greshel

Fallen Sky, Bought and Sold

Collected Poems
by David Greshel

NOMADS, PILGRIMS, TROUBADOURS

DAVID GRESHEL

Windows Into the Past for the Camera Shy

Anniversary Edition

A Poetry Collection
by David Greshel

About the Author/Contact Info

David Greshel is a Mississippi-born, Florida-bred author and poet with a penchant for music, movies, and all things pop culture. Never one to shy away from self-reflection and evaluation, he channels it all into his writing with the results you now see before you.

David currently resides in Palm Bay Florida and can often be found at live music events when not working, writing, or spending time with friends and family.

This is David's fifth collection of poetry. His other collections – Windows into the Past for the Camera Shy, Postcards from a City Ablaze, Nomads, Pilgrims, Troubadours, and Fallen Sky, Bought and Sold - are also available everywhere.

Connect with David:

Email: dgreshel217@gmail.com
Facebook: facebook.com/david.greshel
Instagram/Threads: @electricinfamy
Website: www.neonsunrisebooks.com

NEON SUNRISE
PUBLISHING

Neon Sunrise Publishing is focused on helping independent creators realize their dreams of seeing their books in print. We're driven by a DIY spirit and a desire to provide options and resources to help developing talent succeed in sharing their voice with the world.

To keep up with all of our latest news and releases, be sure to join our mailing list and connect with us online!

Email: neonsunrisepub@gmail.com
Facebook: facebook.com/neonsunrisepub
Instagram: @neonsunrisepub
Website: www.neonsunrisepublishing.com

Made in the USA
Columbia, SC
04 September 2024

f7040019-c30f-4d47-9530-757ac195d37eR01